TO MY MAMA DEAR,
YOU ARE VERY PRECIOUS TO ME..

LOVE,
SELINA

Danny Katz

M.O.T.H.E.R.

Illustrations by Jenny Grigg

HarperCollins*Publishers*

Introduction

Someone recently did a survey in England, trying to find the most beautiful word in the English language. I don't know how you actually do a survey like that, but maybe you just sit a whole bunch of people in a room, start reading through the dictionary and if the people all smile sweetly then that word is considered beautiful, and if the people all start dry-retching violently, maybe that word is not such a big favourite – which could explain why the Beautiful Word List does not contain the words 'pustule', 'curdled' or 'Stan Zemanek'.

Anyway, I won't keep you waiting another moment for the results, because I know the tension is excruciating, so here it is: the winner of the Most Beautiful Word in the English Language … is … 'PUDENDA'. No, not really, I just made that up – but, actually, 'pudenda' is a perfectly nice word, it just rolls off the tongue … Not the pudenda itself – the word … You know what I mean.

No, here's the real winner of the Most Beautiful Word … it's … 'SPLEEN'. No, it's not, but that's also a perfectly good word to say, particularly if you use it in the phrase 'vent your spleen', which sounds like something Freddy Krueger would do to a bunch of college jocks in *Nightmare on Elm Street 12*.

But really, here's the actual winning word, and I'm not kidding any more.

The winner is …

‘MOTHER’.

Yes, that’s right: ‘mother’ was voted the Most Beautiful Word in the English Language and, frankly, I’m a little disappointed – I’m not too thrilled about it, because I think ‘mother’ is a terrible word. I mean, sure, we all love our mothers. I adore mine: she’s a wonderful parent, an incredible teacher, a best friend who has showered me with undying love and devotion and support – but the actual SOUND of the word is hideously ugly. It sounds like ‘the act of being a moth’, or some kind of hip-hop lyric by Snoop Dogg, Hitman and Six-Two about ‘l’il trick-ass mutha ho’s’.

So, while I’m the first person to agree that the MEANING is beautiful and heart-warming, it’s just not a particularly lyrical or gorgeous-sounding word, like 'kinky' or 'squeegee' or 'pig' or 'piggy' or 'piggery' – it's interesting how so many of the best words in the English language are pork-based, unlike the Hebrew language, in which the word 'pig' is pronounced *chazzer* and sounds like an old lady choking on a tennis racket.

If, however, I've got this survey all wrong, and the researchers were only concerned with the MEANING of the word, then sure, there's no question: 'mother' should be right up there at the top of the list, and it should be at the top of all the world's languages, regardless of how the word sounds. In Albania, the word 'mother' is '*kryemurgeshë*', which sounds like the noise your feet would make if you were wading through macaroni. And in the Czech Republic the word 'mother' is '*abatyse*', which sounds more like some kind of super-trendy boutique-style inner-city little abattoir. And in Hawaii, the word for mother is '*makuahine*', which doesn't sound too pleasant at all – it sounds like some kind of medical procedure for a pre-op transsexual.

But mothers give this world its soul, its humanity and its future, so it's a worthy winner. As far as I'm concerned, the top five Most Beautiful Words in the English Language should be 'mother' in first place, closely followed by 'tweezers', and then 'knuckle' and next 'Yasmine' and, finally, 'Bleeth'.

Oh, and 'scrotum' – that's a great word. Can we squeeze 'scrotum' in there too? Not squeeze an actual scrotum – the word. You know what I mean.

Anyway, this is why I've decided to write an entire

book about my mother and mothers in general: I thought it was a really good way to express my eternal gratitude and respect – and also it's the only Mother's Day present I can think of where I get paid for it. So here it is: my book-sized acrostic tribute, where each chapter spells out a letter of the word … 'mother'.

M

Manners

Good manners were always a big deal in our house. If Mum and Dad had guests round for dinner, us kids would always be well-behaved and courteous, and play quietly in our bedrooms until all the guests had gone, then Mum would pop her head in through the door and say, 'Oh kids, I'm so proud of you! You were all so well behaved and wonderful', but we weren't even listening to her – we were too busy racing towards the kitchen, then huddling around the leftovers, and grunting and gnawing and gorging on scraps, with meat juice splattering on our faces, and cartilage spat onto the ground, and bones piling up around us, like some kind of hyena footage from David Attenborough's *Night Creatures of the Kalahari.*

Mottos

Whenever I used to have my school sports carnivals, Mum would always give me a little hug and kiss before I left home, and she'd say, 'Remember, Danny, slow and steady wins the race.' So when it was time for my race I always ran very slowly, and I always kept my body very steady, and I always came about second last. The only kid I ever beat was Mainios Stavrakis, and that's because he had to stop every three metres for a puff of Ventolin.

Mothers-in-law

People make horrible jokes about mothers-in-law and I've never understood it, because I got myself a perfectly nice mother-in-law – she's kind and she's sweet and she thinks I'm immensely gifted because I once changed a lightbulb in her hallway, one of those tricky downlights with the two-pronged globe. Other people don't seem to be so lucky with their mothers-in-law: my friend Gavin, for instance, told me that his wife's mum is as cute as a button – she's small and round and he wants to stick a needle through her.

More motherly mottos …

'Be careful what you wish for, Danny, it just may come true.'

I've never had much luck with this one. I've been doing some pretty heavy wishing since I was fourteen, and I still haven't got that love-sandwich with Kim Wilde and Penelope Pitstop from the *Wacky Races*.

Meatballs – the disgusting Swedish kind

She cooked them in tomato sauce and ginger ale; they were like dense particles from a collapsed star that sucked in all the matter and energy from the universe. Only a little heavier.

Meningococcal

Mum on the phone: 'Did you see that report on TV last night, Danny? There's an outbreak of meningococcal – it's like a plague. I'm just calling because it's serious, you need to keep an eye on the kids, don't let them catch it …'

Music

Mum sent me to guitar lessons when I was a kid. I didn't really want to go to guitar lessons, but Mum thought I had the potential to be a great and gifted songwriter – and it turns out she was right. Here's a poignant little ballad I penned when I was only eleven years old, loosely based on The Beatles' 'Nowhere Man', but only in rhythm and chords and pretty much most of the notes.

JUST A LAD (with plenty of feeling)

```
G              Bm
I was so young
                                   G
C
There was so much to un-der-stand
                                   D
C
Times were rough and times were bad
                                   C          D
G
But then again I was just a lad, Oh yeah!!!
G             Bm          C          G
Oh yeah  oh yeah  oh yeah, oh yeah
G             Bm          C          G
Oh yeah  oh yeah  oh yeah, oh yeah
G             Bm          C          G
Oh yeah  oh yeah  oh yeah, oh yeah (let it build!!!)
      G            Bm          C          G
      Oh yeah  oh yeah  oh yeah, oh yeah (... fade out...)
```

Mum said I was going to be the next Bob Dylan.

Mystery

I've never understood Interflora. You go to the florist's shop, you pick out some flowers for Mother's Day, you ask the florist to send them to your mother in another city, and they get to her the next day. HOW DO THE FLORISTS DO THIS? Do they drive all night and deliver them to her door? Do they freeze them and put them on a plane? And how come I picked out purple gerberas and when they got to her they'd turned orange?

And when you write a little loving message on the Interflora card, why does your handwriting mysteriously change into a whole different style of handwriting by the time it gets to her?

Dan Brown should write a book about this.

Mum at mealtimes

Silence except for the sound of eating.

Mum says, 'Is the chicken all right?' We all say, 'Yeah, it's good', and Mum says, 'Because it's a new recipe, it's Aunty Faigie's recipe, so it may not have worked – it's not my recipe.' Then Dad looks up from his plate and says, 'It's good, I don't know what you're talking about. Just let us eat it. Why do you have to ruin it for us?' Mum says, 'It's good? I'm so relieved. The chicken was tough and greasy when I bought it, and I burned the skin a little when I roasted it. You should've seen the gravy, globby gravy, I had to water it down and strain off the fat …'

Silence except for the sound of eating.

Mum says, 'Who wants gravy?' We all say, 'No, thanks.' My sister asks, 'What's in those bowls over there?' and Mum stands up and points to the bowls: 'Zucchini in this one and potato in this one.' My sister says, 'Pass the zucchini please', and Mum says, 'You don't want any pumpkin?' and my sister says, 'No, I don't feel like pumpkin', and Mum says, 'You should try the pumpkin', and my sister says, 'I don't feel like any pumpkin', and Mum says, 'Try the pumpkin.' So my sister tries the pumpkin and Mum says, 'What about some zucchini? It's Aunty Rae's recipe, it's very nice.'

Silence except for the sound of eating.

We all say, 'Great dinner', and Dad says it in burp-language – 'BRRRRROCHHHHH' – and Mum says, 'Did everyone like the beans? They're Aunty Seale's recipe.' She's carrying dishes to the kitchen and we try to help but she blocks the kitchen door with her short, little, flapping arms – 'NOBODY GOES INTO MY KITCHEN! NOBODY! NOBODY!' – and she makes us sit down. 'Leave it, let me clean up, I enjoy cleaning up by myself. You all enjoy yourselves while I clean up. You relax, don't worry about me, I cook all day for you and now I'll clean up your mess. I LOVE CLEANING UP YOUR MESS.' Then Dad sticks a toothpick in his mouth and mumbles, 'Geez, who invited her?'

Silence except for the sound of cleaning.

Murder!!!

Mothers are obsessed … with murder.

I know this for a fact: my wife and just about all of her mother-friends seem to be into TV crime shows and serial-killer movies and murder-mystery books – any form of entertainment that involves a coroner and a cop and a head that's been severed with a dessert spoon.

It's bizarre – sometimes I hear my wife talking to her sister on the phone and she's saying, 'Did you see last night's episode about the necrophiliac chainsaw-killer? … No, that was after he burned their faces off with a blowtorch … Oh, you mean when he stitched the live birds into her chest cavity?' and I just want to be hiding far, far away, in a cave … in a jungle … in Guatemala …

Memorable Mother's Day presents

1972: A green crocheted clutch-purse that didn't open and cost 17 cents at a Lion's Club Charity Shop.
1985: A black vinyl jacket with heavily padded shoulders – she looked like a coffee table with a head sitting on top.
1986: A pair of acid-washed, marble-washed, stone-washed, pre-mottled, pre-faded, pre-torn jeans that were so baggy around the hips, it looked like she was being inflated from the crotch.
1998: A ceramic thing that may have been a vase, or it may have been a sushi plate – I'm not quite sure, but it was reduced from $59.99 to $19.99 on the Not-Quite-Right Rack.

Mayonnaise

Mum on the phone: 'Danny, don't eat any sandwiches with mayonnaise. I was reading a newspaper story about jars of mayonnaise contaminated with staphylococci. I'm just telling you because I'm concerned about your sandwiches …'

Overpraising

It's only natural that mothers should be proud of their kids, but sometimes it can be a little over the top – a kid could hand their mother a poo on a plate and she'd still get excited about it; she'd say, 'Did you make it yourself? You're SOOOO clever! And on my birthday too!' A kid could clomp someone on the back of the head with a Chinese cleaver and a mum would still run up and hug them and say, 'Darling, you're so talented, one day you're going to be the next Ted Bundy.'

Overcritical

… And at the same time, a mother can shatter your self-esteem in one angstrom of a microsecond. You could discover a cure for pancreatic cancer and your mother would still pull you aside after the Nobel Prize ceremony and say, 'I told you not to wear that suit, it was two sizes too big, the lapels were flapping on your shoulders, the collar was bunching around your neck, your head was sticking out the top like a Chupa Chup …'

Overlenient

I was in the toy department of a big department store and I saw a kid shrieking and howling at his mother because he wanted eighteen different kinds of Spiderman action figure, and as the mother gathered up all the eighteen different kinds of Spiderman action figure and carried them towards the checkout counter, she gave me a pathetic little smile as if to say, 'Why am I doing this?', and I gave her a sympathetic little smile back as if to say, 'Well, I believe it may be a direct outcome of your overlenient permissive parenting, when you choose easy short-term solutions to avoid painful emotional conflict', and she gave me a grateful little smile back as if to say, 'Thank you so much for your extraordinary insight and wisdom. Now will you please stop smiling at me in that creepy way, or I'm going to call Kmart security.'

Overnight …

If I got up in the middle of the night to take a pee, I'd come back to my room and my bed would be made. I think she was hiding behind the door.

Optical matters

My eyes went bad when I was around twelve, so I needed glasses, but I was a highly sensitive, insecure kid, so Mum shopped around in all the trendy spectacle stores and made sure she bought me the coolest, trendiest, most stylish pair of BIG, CHEAP, CLUNKY, PLASTIC-FRAMED GLASSES YOU EVER SAW. These things were like the glasses the optometrist puts on you when you're getting your eyes checked, with all the lenses and levers and latches. But mine were bigger.

Oven in the kitchen

A happy childhood memory: sitting in the kitchen, watching my mother cook dinner. She always seemed to be standing over her oven, baking and roasting and frying. I never saw her face because she always had her back to us – I wasn't even sure what she looked like until she got the kitchen renovated and the stove was moved to the centre bench. And she talked to me as she cooked, telling me stories from her childhood, telling me all the latest family gossip, telling me to stop sticking my fingers into the bowl of chocolate mixture because it wasn't chocolate mixture – it was the hair removal wax she'd been using on her legs that morning.

Orange juice

Mum on the phone: 'Watch out for any kind of packaged orange juice, my friend Jan told me about a batch of packaged orange juice from New Zealand and apparently it was contaminated with salmonella, so don't drink any packaged New Zealand orange juice …'

Other marvellous mottos from my mother

'Look people in the eyes, and don't do the stupid laugh.'

Actually, this one works.

Ohhhhh … Oklahoma!
Where the wind comes sweepin'
down the plain

Oklahoma!, *West Side Story*, *My Fair Lady* … my mother loves musicals. Any kind of musicals. She'd always be playing Broadway cast recordings on the stereo and singing all the roles, and I'd have to stand very quietly beside the couch, because I was the stage manager. Sometimes she'd even spend a whole night communicating in 'musicals language' – at dinner time she'd pop her head out of the kitchen and sing a toe-tapping little production number that goes,

'WHO WANTS A BIT MORE CHICK-EN, I GOT LOTS OF CHICK-EN CHICK-ENNNNN, OH YEAH YEAH YEAHHHHH!'

And us kids would all rise to our feet and sing a big, rousing *Les Mis*–type anthem that goes,

And then we'd hear Dad in the back bathroom singing a 'heartfelt', poignant Rodgers and Hammerstein ballad that goes,

'FOR CHRIST'S SAKE …
WHEN SOMEONE FINISHES A
TOILET ROLL … WILL THEY PLEASE
REPLACE THE BLOODY THING
… AND NOT LEAVE AN EMPTY
CARDBOARD ROLL ON THE TOIL-ET
ROLL HOLDERRRRR'.

Opticals again

Those glasses were so clunky and heavy that Mum had to wrap bits of sponge around the spectacle arms so they didn't slice off my ears.

Olympics according to my mother

'I don't understand the decathlon. Why can't they just have two pentathlons?'

Outdoors

Mum has a serious medical aversion to a specific scientific substance known in academic circles as 'air'. She loves being inside her house, and if I ever leave a door or window open she gets very cross, because I could be contaminating her sterile environment with hazardous external elements like insects, or pollen, or oxygen.

In a perfect world, she would choose to live inside one of those giant sterile bubbles, set up in the middle of her kitchen so she could respire nothing but the smell of smoked salmon, and chicken-schnitzel-frying fumes.

Tough love

I'll never forget my first day of school, because it was a landmark day in my life. Sure, I was a bit sad when Mum left me in my new classroom with my new teacher; sure, there were a few tears, a few whimpers, a few bouts of clawing at the door with my fingernails, yelling, 'DON'T LEAVE ME HERE, MAMA! I DON'T LIKE IT HERE, MAMA! LET ME COME HOME, DON'T LEAVE ME HERE, MAMA … MAMA … MAAAAA-MAAAAA …' but that was just a normal childhood reaction and I got over it very quickly … like, around about the end of fourth grade.

The toilet technique

As far as mothers are concerned, every ailment can be cured by a visit to the toilet: stomach aches, head colds, mouth ulcers, dry and flaky scalps … You could walk into your mother's house holding your own head in your hands after being decapitated by a low-flying French Airbus, and your mum would still yell from the kitchen, 'Did you try sitting on the toilet? You know it'll make you feel better!'

Tough chicken

She put a chicken down in the middle of the table and said, 'Sorry, everyone, but the chicken's a bit rubbery', and Dad said, 'No, I'm sure it's delicious', and Mum said, 'No, I cooked it too long, it's rubbery', and Dad said, 'I'M SURE IT'S NOT RUBBERY', and Mum said, 'But you can hardly cut it, it's so rubbery', and this went on and on until Dad got so annoyed, he picked up the chicken and threw it in the air and the chicken bounced off the ceiling and onto the table, then bounced off the table and onto the carpet, then bounced across the carpet seven or eight times before settling into a nice little dusty place behind the stereo speaker. And Mum said: 'I told you it was rubbery.'

T-shirts

Each year, for the last twenty years, Mum has bought me exactly the same birthday present: a mustard-yellow T-shirt. She seems to think I look terrific in mustard yellow, but everyone else thinks I look sallow and sick, like I just stepped off the Gravitron at Luna Park. So now I've got mustard-yellow T-shirts stuffed in every drawer, hanging on every hanger, chucked up the top of my cupboard, and I don't know what to do with them all. Once I wore one with my pickle-green trousers and I looked like something disgusting that'd been pulled off the top of a cheeseburger.

Travel

There was a famous travel book called *Europe on $5 a Day*, but my mum didn't need that book to know how to travel cheaply – she could've written her own travel book called *The Entire World on $2.50 a Day with Four Kids and a Hungry Husband*, and *You Don't Have to Waste Money Buying that Overpriced Europe on $5 a Day Book*. Here are a few of my mother's terrific travel techniques.

London: The hotels were expensive, so she worked out a way of fitting the whole family in one double bed, with everyone sleeping top to toe, all slotted in together neatly. She got the idea from the $7.99 chicken drumstick value pack from Coles.

z z z z

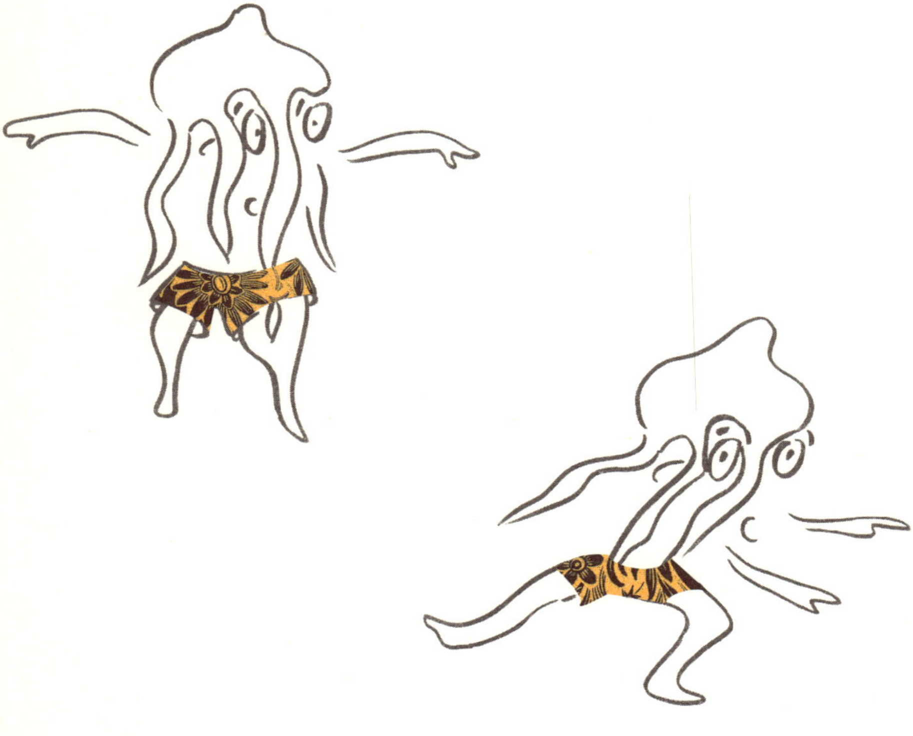

France: Feed the family on nothing but a baguette. No meat. No fruit. Not a vegetable. Just baguettes. Three times a day. We felt full, but we had the energy level of a shoelace.

Sri Lanka: Book a week at the much cheaper beach resort during off-peak season, a resort with quaint little palm trees and quaint little fishing boats and quaint little PORTUGUESE MAN-OF-WAR JELLYFISH WITH TENTACLES AND STINGERS AND HEADS THE SIZE OF LAURIE OAKES. My sister and I got stung so badly that we had to be taken to a medical clinic where a doctor rubbed us with coconut milk for three days, so by the end of our holiday we smelled like a marinated chicken curry. The only thing missing was a bowl of mango chutney.

Tennis no 1

Mum watching the women's tennis on TV: 'Danny, why do all the girl tennis players tuck their tennis balls into their underpants? Why do they do they keep them there? It's disgusting, can't they just put them in their pockets or on the ground or something? I wouldn't want to play with a tennis ball that came from someone's underpants – I wouldn't want to hit that ball if I knew where it had been …'

Tennis no 2

Mum watching the men's tennis on TV: 'You know, you could've been a great tennis player, Danny. Remember when I bought you that toy badminton set and you played with your sister and hit that shuttlecock thing so high in the air that it went on the roof? Oh, you could've been another little Lleyton. Such a waste.'

‘Torrr-mayhhhh-turrrhhhh’

That’s how my mother says the word ‘tomato’. She was born in Canada so she started out saying it with a Canadian accent, but then we moved to Australia, so she tried to say it with an Australian accent, and somehow the two ‘tomatoes’ sort of got mashed together and now it just comes out sounding strangulated and weird, like those automated telephone voices that can’t pronounce your surname. If I go out for lunch with my mother, she always asks for ‘a torrr-mayhhhh-turrrhhhh sandwich and a bowl of poh-tayhhhh-turrrrhhhh chips – and could I get the porrr-tayhhhh-turrrhhhh chips with torrr-mayhhhh-turrrhhhh sauce please?’, and the waiter just stands there staring at her, because he thinks she’s Billy Bob Thornton in *Sling Blade*.

Toothpicks

Mother's Day 1976: We bought her a little wooden native man with a hole in his head for toothpicks.

Tradition

'Bubbie' is the name my kids call my mother; it's an old Jewish word for 'Grandmother' and it's pronounced *Booh-bee.* I don't know the origins of the word, but if you ever see a Jewish grandmother sitting beside a pool wearing a bikini, you'll get a pretty fair idea why they might be called that.

I love all those ethnic names for grandmothers. In Holland they call their grandmothers '*Ooma*', which sounds like something you'd hear in the chorus of a Led Zeppelin song. And in Turkey they call their grandmothers '*Buumlyuumlkanne*', which sounds like a kid trying to say the word 'Grandmother' while his grandmother is force-feeding him a slab of Turkish Delight.

But my favourite grandmother-name of all would have to be the Greek one, '*Yia-Yia*'. It's fun, it's kooky, it's colourful; it sounds like something you'd say to a horse in a Greek cowboy movie: 'YIA-YIAAAAAAA'. Or something you'd hear in a late-night ad for bald Greek grannies: 'Advanced Hair? *Yia-Yia.*'

Teeny-tiny box

Mother's Day 1988: My wife gave her mum a tiny heart-shaped box that was SOOOOO small, the only thing you could fit inside it was an even tinier heart-shaped box.

Teachings of wisdom

'The pen is mightier than the sword': that's what my mother always taught me, and she was right. One time in fifth grade, this bully named Ben Carruthers was teasing me and calling me bad names, and because I was more of a quiet, bookish type, I used the power of the pen: I stabbed him in the arm with it. It was my new ballpoint that I got for my birthday, with the inscription on the side that said, 'To Our Gentle, Sweet Boy – Mum & Dad'.

Telephone calls on weekends

Mum lives in Sydney, I live in Melbourne, and every Saturday morning she calls me and we talk about family, and work, and her amazing new current telephone deal: 'Oh, by the way, Danny, we can have a nice, long chat today because I've got a new long-distance phone deal that only costs 6 cents a minute, with a 16 cent flagfall, if I take advantage of the Weekday Rate Bonus, which is 30 per cent cheaper than the Economy-Bonus Capped-Call Package Offer between 7 a.m. and midnight …' After two hours of talking about her phone deal, the call has cost her $36.

Talking

Mothers love to talk, and they love to talk loudly, and they love to talk about personal kinds of things that other people don't particularly want to hear about. Anyone standing within a 20-metre radius of a group of talking-mums will find out that one recently had a pelvic-floor incident on a trampoline, the other is currently searching the Internet for a herbal thrush remedy, and another is having no luck with her haemorrhoid cream, so she's thinking of switching to suppositories.

House-cleaning on Saturday morning

8.42 a.m. She made the beds. She changed all the sheets, shook out all the doonas, flipped over all the mattresses – and did it really carefully so she didn't wake us up.

9.10 a.m. She put on her bedroom slippers – which were actually a pair of those Pledge Grab-it cloths – and walked around the house, dusting the floor. Those Grab-it cloths are really powerful – she once spent a whole morning dragging round the cat.

9.28 a.m. She sprayed and wiped and vacuumed every room in the house, and we're not talking about half-hearted amateur cleaning – she'd be moving furniture, lifting rugs, ripping the skirting off the wall with a crowbar so she could get to the filth inside the wall cavity.

9.49 a.m. Dad would be reading the paper and he wouldn't be able to stand it any more, he'd yell, 'Geez, cut it out, you're an obsessive cleaning freak, IT'S TIME TO STOP THIS NONSENSE AND TAKE A GOOD, LONG LOOK AT YOURSELF IN THE MIRROR!' So she did – and it was filthy, so she cleaned it with Windex – the new, improved Windex with the anti-streaking formula.

Happiness

Any time I'm feeling sad or hopeless, Mum always knows exactly what to do: she listens to my grievances, she tells me that everything's going to be okay, and then she gives me a little slice of her famous chocolate brownies – and instantly I'm feeling happy and positive again … until I bite into a walnut, and then I'm right back to sad and hopeless. Why do mothers put walnuts in their brownies? Nobody likes walnuts in brownies. It's almost as if they want their kids to be happy, but they don't want their kids to be TOO happy.

Ha ha ha haaaaa hee hee

Another motto – this one is framed and hanging on my mother's kitchen wall, written in flowery needlework. It says …

'It's nice to be important but it's more important to be nice.'

Oh haaaaa haaaaa
heeeee ha ha
Oh right, yeah, sure, Mum, ha ha …

He
Hee hee
Ha haaa

He he Hee
Hee hee
ha ha ha

The horror ...

Here's another one of my original songs; I wrote it back in the summer of 1977 for a girl I had a huge crush on, and for some reason I wrote it in a folky style, loosely based on Paul McCartney's 'Mull of Kintyre', but only in the Scottish feel. And the melody.

THE SOUND OF BELLS (Keep it authentic and Bouncy)

C F C
I can hear the sound of bells

F C
Ringing through the cobbled wells

F Am Dm
And at night the shire hall is shining bright

G C
Where the folk will dance all night

F Dm G
I'd like to take my chance and dance with you

… and then there was a long instrumental bit that I wasn't good enough to play, so I had to hum it instead, and it went 'La-la-laaa la-la-la-laaaaa' over and over again until the song was finished.

Mum said I was going to be the next Simon AND the next Garfunkel.

Happy shoes

Mother's Day 1979: We bought her a pair of those Chinese happy shoes with the rubber soles. She wore them, but she didn't seem very happy.

Hitting

If I ever hit another kid, Mum would hit me back ten times as hard and say, 'No hitting!' Somehow it made sense to her.

Hygienic

I saw a mother sitting at a bus stop with a baby on her lap and the baby was sucking on a dummy, then it spat the dummy onto the ground and the mother bent down and picked up the dummy and put it in her own mouth to sterilise it. She was a really great mum because she didn't want her baby to get sick from the germs on the dirty, filthy ground. The only thing was, she'd just finished smoking a cigarette and had a big, throbbing cold sore on her lip.

Hunger

Mum can whip up an entire meal for a hungry family of six in just three minutes, even though there's nothing in the fridge but a jar of mustard and Dad's toe-rot medicine. She's a superhero with superpowers; we call her Katzwoman, and we just hope she doesn't start wearing a Halle Berry black leather bra-top.

Horses

I've never been crazy about horses. I had a bad experience with a horse when I was a kid – I don't want to go into it right now, only to say that it involved patting a horse on the leg and then finding out that the leg wasn't a leg. Anyway, once Mum took me to a kiddies' fair and put me on a pony ride, and I didn't want to go on the pony – it looked scary. It was one of those evil Shetland ponies with the stumpy legs and the big, brown, placid, gentle, loving eyes. I said, 'NO, MUM, NO!' and Mum said, 'COME ON, IT'S JUST A LITTLE PONY!' and I said, 'I DON'T WANT TO!' and she said, 'COME ON, YOU'RE 14 YEARS OLD, STOP THIS NONSENSE!' – and when she gets like that, you just do it. So I went on the pony ride and my legs dragged along the ground.

Hollywood script no 1

These days everyone's writing a screenplay for a movie. My neighbour Beau is writing a screenplay, my son's dentist is writing a screenplay, MY OWN MOTHER IS WRITING A SCREENPLAY – it's the touching, autobiographical story of a beautiful woman whose kids don't appreciate all the wonderful things she's done for them, with Julia Roberts playing the mother and the kids played by hideous, troll-like George Lucas special effects.

Hollywood script no 2

I'm writing a screenplay, too: it's the touching, autobiographical tale of a mother who phones all of her children just about every single day just to make sure they're all healthy and happy. It's called *Once Were Worriers.*

Hateful children …

It's criminal: children treat their mothers with cruelty and violence and disrespect. You'll see it in supermarkets, on city streets, even in the family home:

seven year olds smacking their mums because they don't want to go to bed; five year olds swearing at their mums because they want some chicken Twisties from the milk bar; BABIES AS YOUNG AS TWO REACHING OUT FROM THEIR PRAMS AND GOING THE PUNCH BECAUSE THEY DON'T WANT TO WEAR THEIR SUNHAT IN THE PARK. And the mothers are not fighting back; they're just standing there, getting whacked and scratched and poked, mumbling gently to their kids, 'Careful, sweetie … OOOOMPH … that hurts Mummy's eye, darling … OOOOOOW … you're making blood come out, pumpkin …'

Homework

A friend recently showed me this: it's her son's fifth grade homework assignment, reprinted word for word …

> Write a theatrical script that shows how a person solves the problem of erosion in their garden. You will need to consider dramatic conventions and provide stage directions and props for your class performance.

Mothers will do anything for their kids, because they want their children to be the best that they can be – so for two whole weeks, in the southern suburbs of Melbourne, a 41-year-old mother with a background in part-time nursing and childcare sat at a kitchen table WRITING A THREE-ACT

PLAY ABOUT EROSION. Night after night she laboured over Brechtian garden-dialogue, she developed gut-wrenching conflict between garden gnomes, and between each scene she stopped to construct a gigantic fake garden out of foam and wood, the likes of which have not been seen since the hydraulic, revolving stage set of *Les Misérables.*

Still getting over that 'nice to be important' thing.

English

She works as a literacy teacher, that's what my mother does for a job: she teaches adults who have trouble reading or writing English, and she's very, very good at it – except now there are probably thousands of Turkish women, and Korean men, and Lebanese people, living all around Australia, using expressions like, 'Excuse me, Mr Greengrocer, could I have a kilo of your nice red torrr-mayhhhh-turrrhhhhs?' and, 'Don't worry, Danny, I'll clean up your mess – you just sit and watch TV, don't worry about me, I LOVE TO CLEAN UP YOUR MESS.'

Eating

My mum's curries are legendary, her pastas are incredible, and her desserts are extremely heavy – by the age of six, I had the cholesterol level of a 300-kilogram prawn.

Economical

Sunday morning brunch: whenever my family all get together, we have bagels at my parents' house. It's a lovely morning with coffee and cheese, and Mum brings out a plate of smoked salmon – it's the biggest plate you've ever seen, but it's got just ten tiny slices of smoked salmon on it, because, at $49.95 a kilo, the stuff costs more than a bus. Then Mum slices the salmon into even smaller portions so everyone can have a bit; this is a procedure that involves a surgical scalpel and an electron microscope. Sometimes the slices are so thin, you can't actually see them; you say, 'Mum, I didn't get any', and she says, 'Yes, you did, you got a HUGE chunk measuring approximately 0.00003582 angstroms.' But the truth is … the truth is, you don't actually need a lot of salmon on your bagel, because the flavour is so intense, you can just rub your hands over the bagel and wipe off the salmon flavour that's still stuck to your fingers from the last brunch.

WELCOME

Entrepreneur

The Baby-At-Home Anti-Burglar Ploy® – my mother is the sole inventor and patent holder. How it works is this: before she goes on a holiday, or a weekend away, or even down to the shops for bread and milk, Mum puts a little handwritten note on the front door that says 'PLEASE KNOCK SOFTLY, BABY ASLEEP', so that burglars will think there's a baby asleep inside and that's why the house is so dark and quiet. This ingenious little psychological deterrent keeps away all kinds of nasty home-intruders, except for Jehovah's Witnesses, who will keep knocking softly at your door for anything up to three days.

Elsa the lioness

She had to carry me out of the cinema during *Born Free* because I got so upset when Elsa the lioness died. I was 14 years old.

Euky Bear Rub

A sick day, home from school: my son is lying in bed, all coughy and phlegmy, rugged up in his favourite Mr Men flannelette jammies, with Mr Grumpy directly over the crotch.

And his mum is there, rubbing eucalyptus cream into his chest like she's oiling up a lamb roast for the oven. Wiping his nose with a tissue because he's created the Eighth Wonder of the World: the Great Hanging Gardens of Mucus. Sitting by his bedside for the whole day, looking all concerned and loving, like it's some big, dramatic intensive-care hospital scene from *ER*.

Electronic equipment

Mothers are not naturally gifted with technology; they don't really know how to wire a hi-fi or configure a computer. My mother-in-law, for example, went into an electrical store and asked the guy there for a 'VD player', and he said, 'Don't you mean a DVD player?' and she said, 'No, it's definitely a VD player, the kind that plays VDs. My friend Judy loves watching VDs, and I want to watch them too.' Eventually the guy sold her a DVD player, but only after he'd convinced her that it was VD-compatible.

Eggs

My daughter still hasn't forgiven her mother for packing that egg sandwich in her school lunchbox on a 34-degree day, so that by lunchtime everyone in the class was pointing at her schoolbag going, 'PEEEEE-YEEEEEWWWWW, THAT STINKS BAD! PEEEEE-YEEEEEWWWWW!' including Mrs Vanderverp, the Reading Recovery Teacher.

Exaggeration!!!

Mum happens to be the most over-the-top exaggerator in the whole country, and the entire world, AND EVERY OTHER PLANET BOTH WITHIN AND BEYOND OUR SOLAR SYSTEM – followed closely by me. Everything Mum says is bigger, better, more amazing than the truth. If she goes to the dentist and gets a cleaning, she comes home and tells us she got a root canal. She burns some porridge in the kitchen, she tells us the house almost caught fire and she was nearly burned alive. She finds a spider in the bathroom, she's running around screaming, 'DON'T WORRY ABOUT ME, YOU SIT AND WATCH TV – I'LL KILL THE FUNNEL WEB ALL BY MYSELF.'

She can't help it; it's a Jewish-mother thing and it's probably been going on for thousands of years. I bet the Red Sea didn't really split in Biblical times – there was probably a little old Jewish mother sitting on the beach and a tiny wave came in and splashed her feet, then she ran home to her husband, yelling, 'Saul, Saul, you won't believe what just happened – I was down at the beach and the Red Sea split in two, just like that. THE WATER PARTED IN THE MIDDLE AND YOU COULD WALK TO THE OTHER SIDE! I'M NOT LYING, SAUL, RIGHT DOWN THE MIDDLE, I TELL YOU!'

The escalating birthday cake paradox

Each time one of us kids had a birthday party, Mum would bake us a personalised birthday cake, and she'd always try to outdo the previous year's birthday cake by a minimum of 80 per cent effort, 90 per cent size, and 100 per cent icing-sugar content. But she was foolish – she started too big, too early: my first birthday cake was a very nice Humpty Dumpty cake with Humpty sitting on a wall; which meant my second birthday cake had to be BETTER, so that was a volcano cake with lava frosting pouring down the side; which meant that my third birthday cake had to be EVEN BETTER STILL, so that was a locomotive cake on a jellybean railway track with blue fairy-floss smoke pouring out of the funnel. This went on and on so that, by the time I was six, she was baking me a 100:1 scale model of a British Bristol World War I Two-Seater Bi-Plane, with wheels and wing-struts, and a front-mounted Lewis gun carved out of a liquorice allsort. The cake looked incredible, but nobody could eat it because it was held together by 300 toothpicks.

Embryo

Swimming has never really been my thing; I'm not a huge swimming sort of guy, and I think it's probably because when I was a kid my mother was terrified of me going in the water. She'd start screaming, 'Don't go in too deep … don't put your head underwater … watch out for the waves' – and then she'd just stand there and watch over me until I finished my bath.

Mum probably didn't even like me being a foetus in her womb: 'Don't put your head under the amniotic fluid … don't swim too close to the uterine lining … you've just finished eating, so sit on the placenta for half an hour before going back in.'

E-coli

Mum on the phone: 'Just calling to say don't make contact with farm animals, I was listening to the radio and there's an outbreak of *Escherichia coli*, so if you HAVE to be in contact with farm animals – and I don't know why you would, but if you must be – DON'T touch their manure, and if you need to touch it, for whatever reason – I don't want to know – wash your hands with soap …'

Eeeee-yewwwww

It was kind of weird: she used to dust the furniture with our old, unwanted undies. One time I said to her, 'Mum, is that hygienic? I mean, you're wiping down the dining room table!' and she said, 'It's fine, I washed them, they're clean – now, hand me your father's old yellow Y-fronts, I want to give the cutlery a bit of a shine.'

Enemies

Mum has none; everyone adores her. She once said to me, 'Danny, if you make at least five really good friends in your life, then you're doing all right.' She has 500. I have two.

And they both like her more.

R

Rib-tickling jokes

Mum telling a joke: 'There are two old ladies, and they go into a food shop, like a café – I don't know, who cares. So they say to the waiter, "Can I have a drink, please?" – did I mention there's a waiter? Yeah, there's a waiter, and they ask for a clean glass – I think that's right. So the waiter comes back with a glass – did I mention there's a waiter? Anyway, the punchline is this: he says, "Take this glass and clean it yourself." No – he says, "Who wanted a clean glass?"

'How does it go again?'

Then Mum turns to Dad and says, 'You tell it.'

Road inventions

The Lane-Changing Radar-Sonic-Televisual-Sonic Thingie® – she came up with the concept and owns the intellectual rights. See, there are so many drivers out there – just like her – who dread having to change lanes. She usually gets into a lane and tries to stay there for her whole journey, which may be why she often drives around in circles. So that's why she's proposing a device built into the dashboard that can warn the 'lane-timid driver' if there's any other car in, say, a 5-kilometre radius – then she (or he) can easily change lanes without fear or stress. YES, IT SEEMS SO OBVIOUS NOW.

Rubbing tummies

Stomach problems can always be fixed by a mother's patented rubbing technique: round and round, up and down … and … somehow … oh my God … it works! Professional doctors should try out this brilliant technique on their patients: 'I'm sorry, Mr Macintyre, I'm afraid you've got chronic ulcerative colitis, but you don't need surgical treatment – here, lift your shirt … and … rubbing round and round … up and down … and see, all better, all better. And now, a widdle tummy kiss on your widdle tum-tum! So, will that be Medicare or private?'

Really sweet ...

Yesterday my daughter baked cookies with her mother. They got out the little duck-shaped cookie-cutters from the kitchen drawer and my girl cut out the cookie shapes and decorated them with Smarties and popped them in the oven, then sweet baking-cookie smells started wafting around the house, lifting my heart, making me feel warm and wonderful and loving and happy … until I stepped on a cookie-cutter in my bare feet and left little duck-shaped footprints of blood up and down the kitchen floor.

Rolos

Some people have searched for the Lost City of El Dorado, others have sought out the Holy Grail of Christ, but me, I've dedicated my life to finding My Mother's Hidden Packet of Nestlé's Rolo Chocolates, those delicious round treats with the gloopy caramel inside. She's got them hidden somewhere in the house, and she enjoys them daily while the rest of the family have to settle for tiny scraps of cooking chocolate from the back of the pantry that are so old and bitter even the ants walk around them.

Records

I bought my first album when I was 15 years old: it was Skyhooks' *Livin' in the '70s* and I sang all the songs around the house – 'Horror Movie', and 'Balwyn Calling', and 'You Just Like Me Cos I'm Good In Bed' – but I didn't want to upset my mum, so I changed the words to 'You just like me cos I make my bed'.

Reminiscing ...

Mother's Day 1982: Mum wanted a family photo as a present, which sort of annoyed us, because we thought the purple paisley leggings and the *Xanadu* soundtrack were more than enough. But, anyway, she wanted a photo that really captured the true essence of the Katz family, so she took us to a photographer who specialised in novelty shots, and he dressed us up in 18th-century English outfits and made us stand against a backdrop of a stately English manor, and made us pose in a stern-faced, unhappy way – because apparently everyone was in those days – and that was the photo we got: a sepia-toned portrait of a bunch of miserable Canadian Jews, comprising my father in top hat and cape looking like a Semitic Mr Magoo, my mother in a gown and tiara looking like Barbra Streisand at Ascot, and the four of us kids in sailor suits with pompoms and bows looking almost like the Huey, Dewey and Louie of Tel Aviv.

Rancid

Mother's Day 1978: we bought her a bottle of Charlie, which was a cheap brand of perfume that smelled like a tub of scented baby wipes.

Repulsive

Here's a song I wrote when I was only 16 years old. It was a slow, bluesy number loosely based on Ray Charles's 'Hit the Road Jack', with a commercial, poppy feel loosely based on Billy Joel's 'She's Always A Woman'. And it was going to be the big, rousing love theme of my new, ultra-modern Biblical rock opera, loosely based on *Jesus Christ Superstar*, called … *Shelumiel, Son of Zurishaddai.*

MORNING MALKA

(andante, and also Allegro, and also a bit Larghetto in the middle bit)

```
C                 F           C
Morning, Morning, Malka

C            Am                   F - G
You bake your bread in the morning

   Am              Em
You knead with your fingers

   F                  C
And powder the table

C       F                     Dm
That's when I love you the most

F                  G                      C
In the morning... when you bake your bread!
```

Mum threatened to cancel my guitar lessons.

JENNY GRIGG

Respect

These days, kids are in charge and parents can't tell them to do anything – you ask your kid to brush their teeth and the next thing you know, they've made a couple of calls and you're getting carted off by Community Services. But when I was a kid, I treated my mother with respect and honour and TOTAL, ABSOLUTE FEAR. I did everything I was told – 'Sure, Mum, I'll clean the toilet for you. What? No scrubbing brush? Okay, I'll do it with my fingernails.'

Returning

Some people climb mountains to get their thrills; some people sail oceans to get a buzz; some people jump out of aeroplanes for a few heart-stopping kicks – but my mother gets her adrenaline rush in a badder, bolder, braver way: on weekends she dresses up in her sporty gear, puts on her running shoes, then heads off to indulge in the most extreme sport of all … She goes to the department store and returns stuff she bought the week before.

NOBODY returns stuff like she can. She doesn't get scared, she just goes straight up to the girl at the counter, keeps a steady gaze and says, 'I'd like to return this item' – SHE DOESN'T EVEN SAY 'PLEASE'. And if the girl asks her why she wants to return it, my mother doesn't turn around and run out; she says, 'Because it doesn't suit me, that's all.' The woman is fearless and focussed and fast – SHE'S THE MICHAEL SCHUMACHER OF SHOPPING.

Rude language

My mother dropping a plate:
'Oh, shoot.'

My mother stubbing her toe on the coffee table:
'Owww … shoot!'

My mother on fire: 'AHHHHHH … AHHHHH … AH
HHHHHHHHHHHHHHHHHHHHHHHHHHHHH
HHHHHHHHHHHHHHH … shoot … AHHHHHHH
AHHHHHHHH!'

Recipes

If a meal works, it's her recipe. If it doesn't, it's Aunty Eve's.

Radiance

She's incredible; she turned 63 this year and seems to be getting younger and more beautiful as the years go on – although she's getting smaller, so by the time she hits 70 she'll look great … and she'll also be able to stand on her own birthday cake and hold up the decorations.

Put them all together, they spell

MOT

HER

… and also, thank you, Mum, for teaching me how to spell.

HarperCollins*Publishers*
First published in Australia in 2006
by HarperCollins*Publishers* Australia Pty Limited
ABN 36 009 913 517
www.harpercollins.com.au

HarperCollins*Publishers*
25 Ryde Road, Pymble, Sydney, NSW 2073, Australia
31 View Road, Glenfield, Auckland 10, New Zealand
77-85 Fulham Palace Road, London, W6 8JB, United Kingdom
2 Bloor Street East, 20th floor, Toronto, Ontario M4W 1A8, Canada
10 East 53rd Street, New York NY 10022, USA

National Library of Australia Cataloguing-in-Publication data:

Katz, Danny.
M.O.T.H.E.R.
ISBN 0 7322 8285 3.
1. Motherhood – humor. 2. Mothers – humor.
I. Grigg, Jenny (Jenny A.). II. Title.
306.87430207

Cover and internal design by Jenny Grigg
Mid-nineteenth century wood-engraved ornamented types of end grain boxwood, now in the collection of the St Bride Printing Library, appeared in *Letterpress: the Allure of the Handmade* by David Jury, Rotovision Publishers 2004.
Typeset in 12.5/17.5pt Berthold Baskerville
Printed and bound in China by Pheonix Offset Printing 100gsm Munken Print

5 4 3 2 1 06 07 08 09

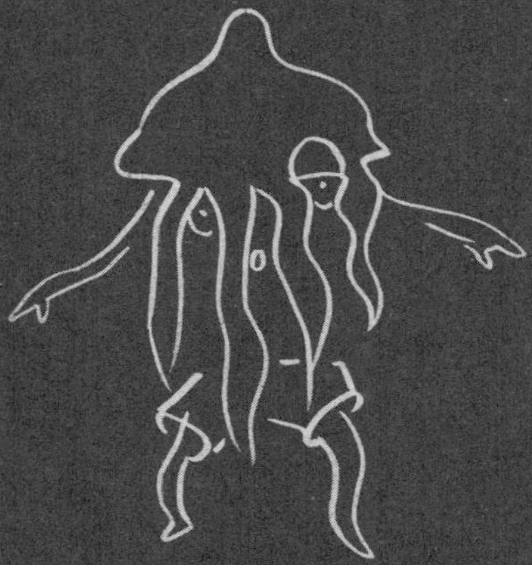

About the Author

Canadian-born Danny Katz emigrated to Australia at a young age because his geologist father felt there were interesting rocks here. Danny worked as a car washer, a leather belt salesman and a musical composer before stumbling into stand-up comedy, where he made his name in the 1990s. He is a columnist for the *Sydney Morning Herald*, *The Age* and the *West Australian.*

Danny lives in Melbourne with his wife and two children, and is the author of *Spit the Dummy*, *Dork Geek Jew* and several children's books, including the *Little Lunch* series.